Just Like Me!

by Damian Harvey

Illustrated by Federica Nuccio and Roberta Vottero

Notes on the series

TIDDLERS are structured to provide support for children who are starting to read on their own. The stories may also be used for sharing with children.

Starting to read alone can be daunting. **TIDDLERS** help by listing the words in the book for a check before reading, and by providing visual support and repeating words and phrases. These books will both develop confidence and encourage reading and rereading for pleasure.

If you are reading this book with a child, here are a few suggestions:

1. Make reading fun! Choose a time to read when you and the child are relaxed and have time to share the story.
2. Talk about the story before you start reading. Look at the cover and the blurb. What might the story be about? Why might the child like it?
3. Look also at the list of words below – can the child tackle most of the words? Encourage the child to employ a phonics approach to tackling new words by sounding the words out.
4. Encourage the child to retell the story, using the jumbled picture puzzle.
5. Give praise! Remember that small mistakes need not always be corrected.

Here is a list of the words in this story.

Common words:

a	just	me
and	like	this
big	looks	to
I	love	
is	loves	

Other words:

elephant	monkey	silly
giraffe	oops!	taking
having	pictures	tall
lion	roar	wash

"I love taking pictures!"

"This elephant is having a wash."

4

"This lion loves to roar."

"Just like me!"

"This giraffe is big and tall."

12

13

"Just like me!"

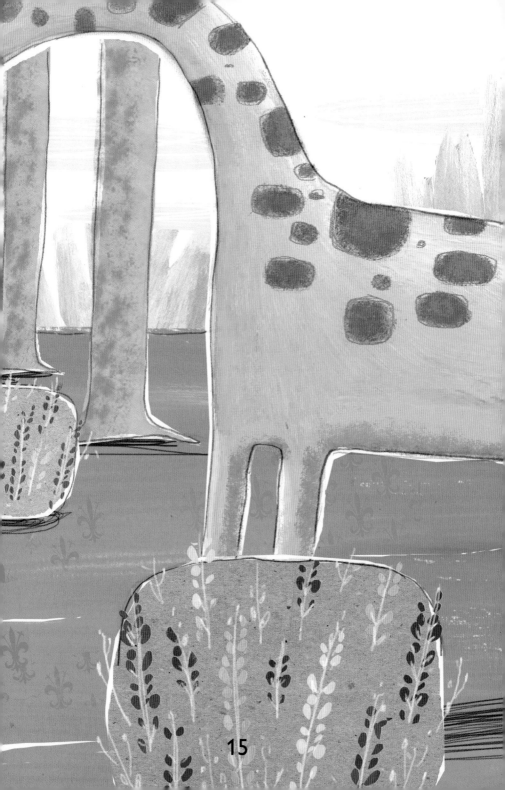

"This monkey looks silly."

"Just like me!"

Puzzle Time

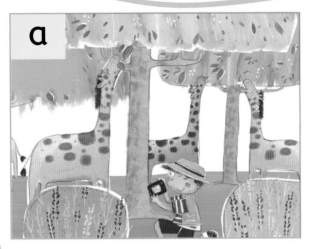

Can you find these
pictures in the story?

Which pages are the
pictures from?

Turn over for answers!

Answers

The pictures come

from these pages:

a. pages 12–13

b. pages 18–19

c. pages 4–5

d. pages 8–9

Franklin Watts
First published in Great Britain in 2016 by
The Watts Publishing Group

Copyright (text) © Damian Harvey 2016
Copyright (illustration) © Federica Nuccio
and Roberta Vottero 2016

The rights of Damian Harvey to be
identified as the author and Federica Nuccio
and Roberta Vottero to be identified as the
illustrators of this Work have been asserted
in accordance with the Copyright, Designs
and Patents Act, 1988.

Series Editor: Jackie Hamley
Series Advisor: Catherine Glavina
Series Designer: Cathryn Gilbert

A CIP catalogue record for this book is
available from the British Library.

ISBN 978 1 4451 4601 0 (hbk)
ISBN 978 1 4451 4603 4 (pbk)
ISBN 978 1 4451 4602 7 (library ebook)

Printed in China

Franklin Watts
An imprint of
Hachette Children's Group
Part of The Watts Publishing Group
Carmelite House
50 Victoria Embankment
London EC4Y 0DZ

An Hachette UK Company
www.hachette.co.uk

www.franklinwatts.co.uk

**Love and thanks to Vicky for this
story idea – D.H.**

FSC
www.fsc.org
MIX
Paper from
responsible sources
FSC® C104740